Falling in Love with Loneliness

Finley Rose

Presentation by *BookLeaf Publishing*

Web: www.bookleafpub.com

E-mail: info@bookleafpub.com

ISBN: 9789360944452

First edition 2024

For the lonely hearts learning to love again.

ACKNOWLEDGEMENT

I want to start by saying thank you to my parents, Joni and Dave. Thank you for being supportive in my journey of becoming a writer and encouraging me to step outside of my comfort zone and explore new ways of writing and getting people to read my work. Thank you for trusting me to pursue this path and for your love along the way.

Secondly, the biggest thank you goes to my best friend, Kendra. Thank you for sending me this project and encouraging me to go for it. I am beyond grateful for all of your love, support, and editing skills throughout my writing journey. Your brutal honesty is usually right most of the time and I am so thankful for it. I love telling you about my projects because of how excited you get and it makes me more excited to continue this writing journey.

Thank you to my first readers who have told me how to fix, edit, and revise my work. A special thank you to Erin Tiede, Alyssa Arnold, and Jessica Lindsay for planting my writing seed and helping it to grow and thrive beyond the walls of high school.

Thank you to BookLeaf Publishing which has allowed me to put out this collection for people to read!

It's Hard to Love the Silence

It's hard to love the silence
when all you know is noise.

It's hard to love the peace
when all you know is war.

It's hard to love the praise
when all you know is criticism.

It's hard to love yourself
when all you know is others.

Too Early // Too Late

The timelines of our love were never aligned.

You fell first but I fell fast
and when it reached the end
you were done loving me,
but I wasn't quite done loving you.

You loved me too early
and I loved you too late,
and now I have to lay here
in the solemn silence
of my lonely heartbreak.

The Movie Kind of Love

I want a movie kind of love.

The kind of love that
kisses and dances in the
rain as soft music plays
without a care in the world.

The kind of love that spells
"I'm Sorry" in M&Ms on
pizza and causes my foot to
pop after the first kiss.

The kind of love where
he stands with a boombox
over his head playing "In
Your Eyes" at midnight.

The kind of love where
he doesn't forget that I'm
just a girl standing in front
of a boy asking him to love me.

The kind of love where
we want all of each
other, forever, him
and me, every day.

Deliberate Heartbreak

With you, falling in love is
the most deliberate heartbreak
because I know never in a million
years could you ever love me back.

But still I long for your strong arms
around me and your lips pressed
against my forehead as you hold
me close in the quiet of the night.

Over

5

I am over
feeling
like I can't
talk about
how I'm
truly feeling
about you
and me
and us.

I am over
only talking
when it's
convenient
for you and
when you
need me
and my
heart.

I am over
feeling self-
conscious
when I finally
talk about
me and you
turn it
around
on you.

I am over it.
I'm just done.

Always the Poet

Always the poet, never the poem.
The one with the all words,
always longing to be the observed.

Always the lover, never the loved.
The one with the big open heart,
always longing to be the one they want.

Always the bridesmaid, never the bride.
The one with the tears in here eyes,
always longing to find her guy.

Always the needed, never the wanted.
The one with the listening ears,
always longing not to be left in tears.

'Lonely'

I feel a different kind of 'lonely' with you.
It's not sad, but it's not happy.
It's not comfortable, but not uncomfortable.
It's like there's peace in my brain but war in my
heart,
and we are the one's standing on the battlefield.
Lonely in our goals, our thoughts,
but together in our fears, our doubts,
neither one of us wanting to be the first to shoot.

Island

I wanted to like today but I couldn't.
We were sitting in the same room,
walking down the same path,
sitting in the same car,
and yet we couldn't be further apart,
like two lone islands,
that were once connected,
but now had to separate hearts.

Right Person, Wrong Time

I never believed in right person, wrong time

until I fell in love you,

then out of love with you,

but still my heart stayed with you.

I Wish I Wasn't So...

I wish I wasn't so
acquainted with the
feeling of loneliness.

I wish I wasn't so
familiar with my own
company on Friday nights.

I wish I wasn't so
okay spending my time
alone than with others.

I wish I wasn't so
introverted since the
world shut down.

I wish I wasn't so
reserved and was able
to put myself out there.

But what I really wish is that
I wasn't so hard on myself to
be as social as I once was.

I Have Big Feelings

I have big feelings which means
I feel a lot of things all at once.

It means two words could send me
down the rabbit hole of depression.

It means your tone of voice could put
me on edge for every future conversation.

It means one little thing could go wrong
and I could blow up like a ticking bomb.

I have big feelings which means
I feel a lot of things all at once.

It means that sunshine puts the biggest
smile on my face that is hard to go away.

It means that the smallest compliment
can make me giddy for a whole week.

It means that laughter is my favorite
cure for any sadness inside of me.

I have big feelings which means
I feel a lot of things all at once.

It means that memories stay with me
so I can feel everything again and again and
again.

All I Wanted To Do Was Love You

All I wanted to do was love you.
To care for you and hold you and want you.
But you wanted nothing to do with me.
You discarded me like some toy you were done
playing with.
Now I'm alone,
learning to love myself like you never could.

My Turn

I'm waiting.
I'm waiting for it to be my turn.

My turn to fall in deep, deep love.
Love like the books.
Love like the movies.
Love that I've dreamed of
since I was seven years old.

I want it to be my turn.
I'm ready for it to be my turn.

Befriending Devils

"Tell me every terrible thing you ever did,
and let me love you anyway." - Edgar Allen Poe

I want to befriend the devil on your shoulder,
and show him the love that he was never shown.

I want to see your deep, dark pits of sadness,
and fill them with the golden truth of happiness.

I want to carry you when you feel too heavy,
and walk with you until you see the light of hope.

I want to love you through the darkness of life,
and even more through the light parts too.

But that can never happen because my devils, pits,
weights, and darkness are all too much for you.

Somewhere Between Friends and Lovers

We're somewhere between friends and lovers.
Our glances hold a little bit longer.
Our shoulders brush a little bit more.
Our voices are a little bit quieter.

But it never moves beyond that.
The boundary stays strong.
But sometimes, sometimes
Sometimes I wish it was gone.

Untitled

She's prettier than me.

I never thought I'd say that
about anyone, but she is.

Her long, beautiful hair pulls
off the colors better than me.

Her big, brown eyes wear
the make-up better than me.

Her bright, happy smile is filled
with more joy than mine.

Especially when she looks at you.

Even more so when you look back.

Wonderland

I hate to be left alone with my wandering mind,
but where else am I supposed to find myself?

It's a beautiful wonderland of undiscovered
mysteries,
all teaching me to love my heart more and more.

My best ideas have come to me in that utopia:
worlds of dreams, fairies, love, and magic.

So please leave me alone with my wandering mind,
so I can create the new world you will soon fall in
love with.

The Best Company

Lonely people make for the best company

because they do not care what your mind

is doing, just that your heart is beating and

you're there fighting battles next to them.

Cherish

I cherish those that listen because
they have the most beautiful minds.

I cherish those that care because
they have the most kind hearts.

I cherish those that are lonely because
they see the world in the most brilliant way.

I cherish those that are hurting because
they have won the most battles.

I cherish those that are happy because
they have sunshine in their souls.

I cherish you
and her
and him
and them
and me.

I cherish me.

Over and Over Again

A great relationship is about
falling in love with the same
person over and over again.

I choose my own company and
hobbies over the habits of
others over and over again.

I write my own words and have
grown to appreciate the familiarity
of my voice over and over again.

I listen to my own heartbeat and
breathing and compose a gentle
symphony over and over again.

I have fallen in love with being
myself over and over again.

I Fell in Love with the Loneliness

I fell in love with the loneliness.
The beauty in quiet,
the peace in my heartbeat,
the white noise of my breathing.

I fell in love with the pain of mourning,
the "goodbyes" that felt neverending.
Even if I never got to say them,
their presence always loomed over me.

I fell in love with the solo recital.
My voice has never felt more familiar,
echoing off the cement walls,
flooding my senses from every angle.

Finally, I fell in love with my heart.
My mind, my soul.
They work in tandem now,
better than ever before.